FOOTBALL
ACTIVITY BOOK FOR KIDS

FREE FOOTBALL GAME INSIDE!!

Elliott Frost

Publisher information

Published by Elliott Frost books

Copyright (c) 2023 Elliott Frost

This book belongs to:

Ari

Looking for even more fun?

Use the QR Code below to gain access to even more free fun activities.

FOOTBALL
ACTIVITY BOOK
FOR KIDS

Anagrams #1

Rearrange letters for names of Premier League Teams

ERVPOLLOI

....

NNWOUTLOT

....

TUHEORBONUM

....

ETHANTMOT

...Tottenham................................

Wordsearch #1

P	G	U	P	Q	S	W	E	M	Z	X	B	F	R
E	Z	S	B	A	H	I	N	B	R	Y	E	N	M
T	L	A	X	R	U	B	G	D	M	V	J	U	T
H	U	Y	N	G	W	R	L	W	D	O	Y	K	P
Q	M	M	L	E	S	A	I	B	F	V	V	V	V
S	P	A	I	N	D	Z	N	W	P	R	O	Q	U
N	K	N	X	T	O	I	D	B	O	A	M	V	U
N	B	E	L	I	K	L	Q	L	R	N	E	Q	E
U	M	S	N	N	I	C	C	C	T	C	T	N	R
B	S	C	T	A	Q	Z	D	X	U	E	F	S	J
S	R	R	L	S	A	W	I	O	G	X	C	O	P
O	C	N	I	T	A	L	Y	P	A	R	E	X	R
D	Q	O	A	U	S	T	R	A	L	I	A	I	L
Y	R	G	E	R	M	A	N	Y	D	J	W	Q	Z

USA ✓
FRANCE ✓
GERMANY ✓
AUSTRALIA ✓

ITALY ✓
BRAZIL ✓
PORTUGAL ✓

SPAIN ✓
ENGLAND ✓
ARGENTINA ✓

7

Wordsearch Solution

P	G	U	P	Q	S	W	E	M	Z	X	B	F	R
E	Z	S	B	A	H	I	N	B	R	Y	E	N	M
T	L	A	X	R	U	B	G	D	M	V	J	U	T
H	U	Y	N	G	W	R	L	W	D	O	Y	K	P
Q	M	M	L	E	S	A	A	I	B	F	V	V	V
S	P	A	I	N	D	Z	N	W	P	R	O	Q	U
N	K	N	X	T	O	I	D	B	O	A	M	V	U
N	B	E	L	I	K	L	Q	L	R	N	E	Q	E
U	M	S	N	N	I	C	C	C	T	C	T	N	R
B	S	C	T	A	Q	Z	D	X	U	E	F	S	J
S	R	R	L	S	A	W	I	O	G	X	C	O	P
O	C	N	I	T	A	L	Y	P	A	R	E	X	R
D	Q	O	A	U	S	T	R	A	I	A	I	L
Y	R	G	E	R	M	A	N	Y	D	J	W	Q	Z

USA	ITALY	SPAIN
FRANCE	BRAZIL	ENGLAND
GERMANY	PORTUGAL	ARGENTINA
AUSTRALIA		

Colouring Page #1

BLANK FOR COLOURING PAGE

Colouring Page #2

BLANK FOR COLOURING PAGE

Design a team shirt badge

Team Name: Hartleport City FC

Team Nickname: Doves

Stadium Name: Mitre Stadiem

Star Player:

Make a Football design

The World Cup Final needs a special ball.
Use your imagination and design one.

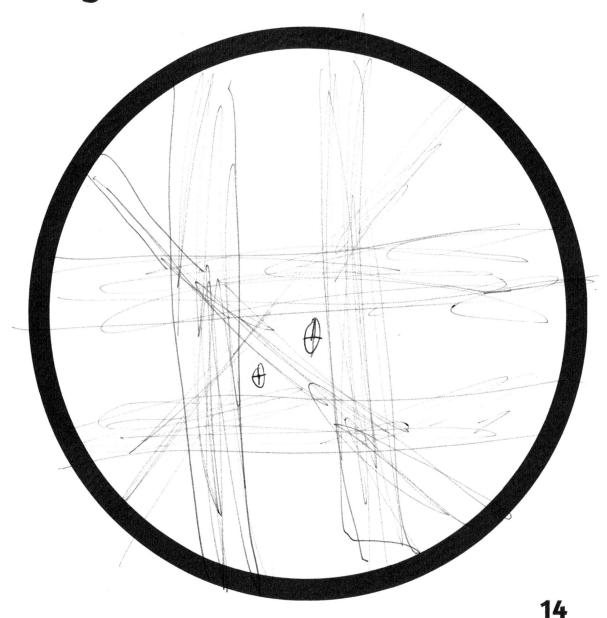

Ultimate Team!!

Write down your favourite players (1 keeper, 4 defenders, 4 midfielders and 2 strikers)

Hartlepool City FC

HCFC

erling Haaland	Eric Cantona
NOR	FRA

Alejandro Garnacho	Frenkie De Jong	Lothar Mathäus	Zinedin Zidane
ARG	NER	GER	FRA

Roberto Carlos	nemanja Vidić	Fabio Cannavaro	Trent Alexander-arnold
BRA	SRB	ITA	ENG

ley Yashin
USSR

Favourites!

Answer each question with your favourite answers:

Favourite Club Team: Man United

Favourite Club Player: Alejandro Garnacho

Who do they play for? United

What do you like about them? Bicycle kick V Everton

Favourite League? Premier

What team do you play for? London United Football School (CLUFS)

What position do you play? CAM

If you could play Football in the future, who would you like to play for? Man U

Colouring Page #3

BLANK FOR COLOURING PAGE

Colouring Page #4

BLANK FOR COLOURING PAGE

Colouring Page #5

BLANK FOR COLOURING PAGE

Word Search #2

W	O	P	G	S	S	Z	U	F	H	G	E	S	X	R
G	Z	F	S	U	T	K	N	Q	T	O	I	U	A	O
X	Z	Z	O	B	R	E	X	T	R	A	T	I	M	E
N	Z	Q	I	S	I	Y	R	A	L	L	H	N	X	E
L	F	P	Q	T	K	M	M	P	P	K	G	E	J	J
M	I	D	F	I	E	L	D	E	R	E	G	Y	G	C
L	D	X	Q	T	R	D	P	N	Z	E	K	J	O	B
J	E	T	I	U	S	D	X	A	T	P	X	P	A	V
C	F	P	V	T	W	E	H	L	D	E	U	P	L	X
C	E	W	L	E	Y	R	L	T	C	R	B	U	P	L
M	N	H	H	A	L	F	T	I	M	E	Z	Z	O	T
C	D	U	U	R	H	Z	K	E	O	X	I	G	S	G
W	E	G	T	V	S	Z	G	S	C	N	H	C	T	S
R	R	R	H	O	X	E	N	T	C	K	G	M	W	U
X	N	M	G	O	A	L	H	T	O	Z	E	D	F	H

GOAL
HALF TIME
GOALKEEPER
EXTRA TIME

STRIKER
PENALTIES
MIDFIELDER

DEFENDER
GOAL POST
SUBSTITUTE

Word Search Solution

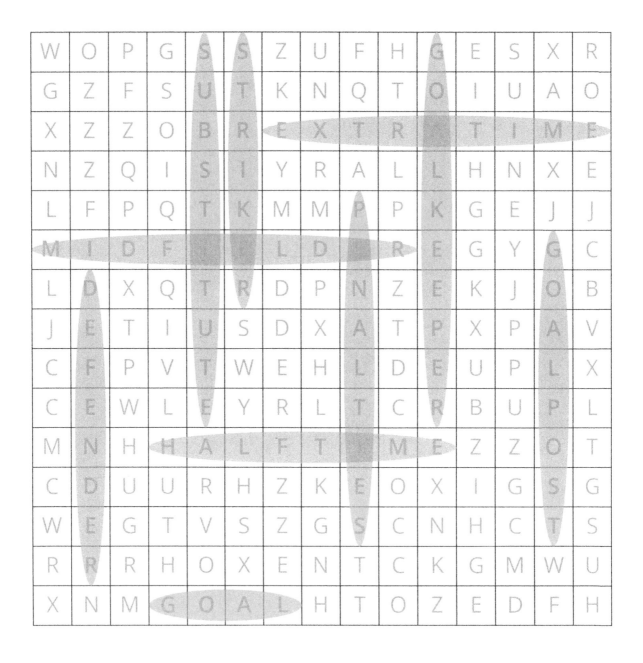

W	O	P	G	G	S	S	Z	U	F	H	G	E	S	X	R
G	Z	F	S	U	T	K	N	Q	T	O	I	U	A	O
X	Z	Z	O	B	R	E	X	T	R	A	T	I	M	E
N	Z	Q	I	S	I	Y	R	A	L	L	H	N	X	E
L	F	P	Q	T	K	M	M	P	P	K	G	E	J	J
M	I	D	F	I	E	L	D	E	R	E	G	Y	G	C
L	D	X	Q	T	R	D	P	N	Z	E	K	J	O	B
J	E	T	I	U	S	D	X	A	T	P	X	P	A	V
C	F	P	V	T	W	E	H	L	D	E	U	P	L	X
C	E	W	L	E	Y	R	L	T	C	R	B	U	P	L
M	N	H	A	L	F	T	I	M	E	Z	Z	O	T
C	D	U	U	R	H	Z	K	E	O	X	I	G	S	G
W	E	G	T	V	S	Z	G	S	C	N	H	C	T	S
R	R	R	H	O	X	E	N	T	C	K	G	M	W	U
X	N	M	G	O	A	L	H	T	O	Z	E	D	F	H

GOAL
HALF TIME
GOALKEEPER
EXTRA TIME

STRIKER
PENALTIES
MIDFIELDER

DEFENDER
GOAL POST
SUBSTITUTE

Crossword #1

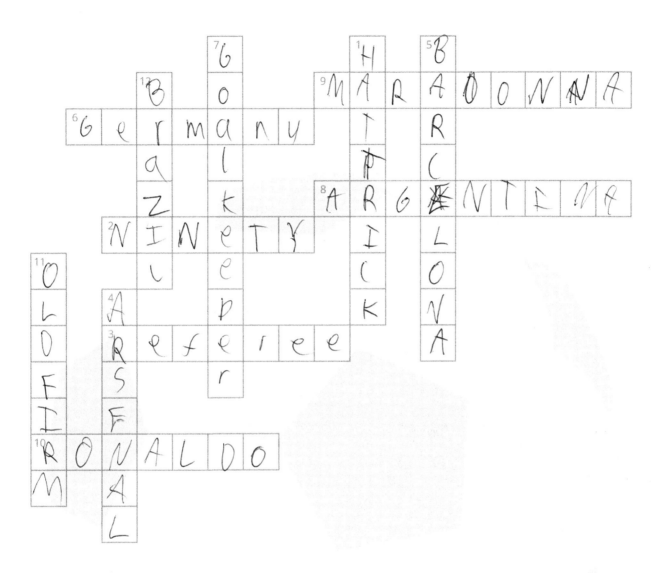

Across
2. NUMBER OF MINUTES IN A FOOTBALL MATCH?
3. PERSON WHO OFFICIATES THE GAME?
6. WHO WON THE 2014 FIFA WORLD CUP?
8. WHICH COUNTRY DOES LIONEL MESSI COME FROM?
9. WHO IS OFTEN CALLED THE 'HAND OF GOD' SCORER?
10. WHO IS KNOWN AS 'CR7' IN THE FOOTBALL WORLD?

Down
1. IF A PLAYER SCORES THREE GOALS,WHAT IS IT CALLED?
4. WHICH ENGLISH TEAM IS KNOWN AS THE GUNNERS?
5. IN WHICH CITY IS THE STADIUM KNOWN AS THE 'CAMP NOU'?
7. WHAT POSITION DOES ALISSON BECKER PLAY?
11. NAME OF THE RANGERS V CELTIC GAME
12. WHICH COUNTRY DOES NEYMAR COME FROM?

Crossword #1 Solution

Across
2. NUMBER OF MINUTES IN A FOOTBALL MATCH?
3. PERSON WHO OFFICIATES THE GAME?
6. WHO WON THE 2014 FIFA WORLD CUP?
8. WHICH COUNTRY DOES LIONEL MESSI COME FROM?
9. WHO IS OFTEN CALLED THE 'HAND OF GOD' SCORER?
10. WHO IS KNOWN AS 'CR7' IN THE FOOTBALL WORLD?

Down
1. IF A PLAYER SCORES THREE GOALS,WHAT IS IT CALLED?
4. WHICH ENGLISH TEAM IS KNOWN AS THE GUNNERS?
5. IN WHICH CITY IS THE STADIUM KNOWN AS THE 'CAMP NOU'?
7. WHAT POSITION DOES ALISSON BECKER PLAY?
11. NAME OF THE RANGERS V CELTIC GAME
12. WHICH COUNTRY DOES NEYMAR COME FROM?

Maze

The Bus Driver is lost!! Help him find the Football Stadium

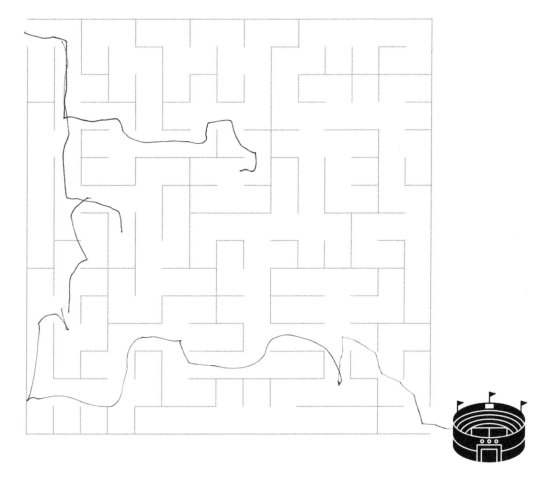

Maze Solution

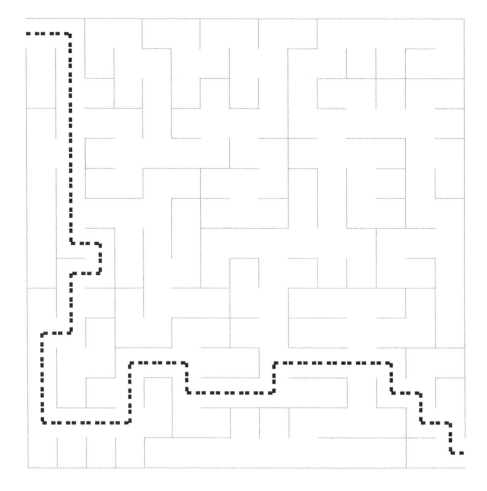

Football Hangman

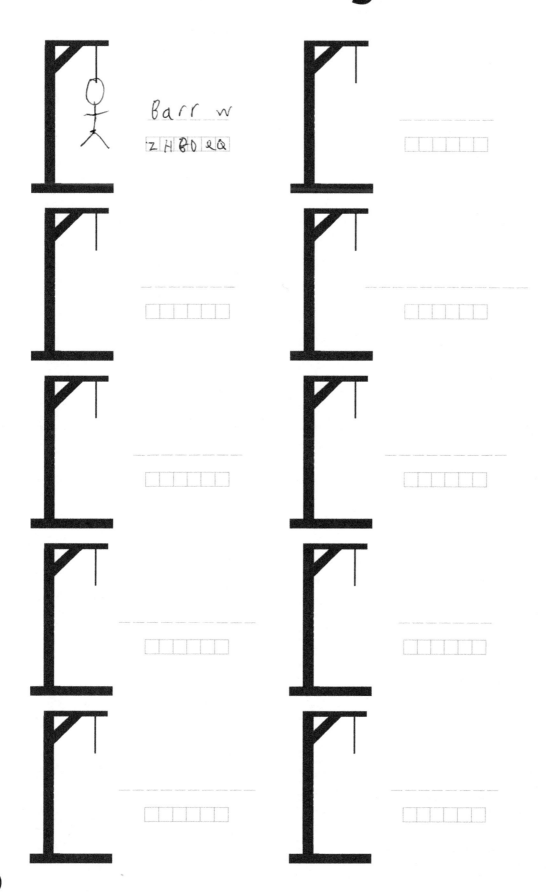

Barr w

ZHBOQQ

Football Hangman

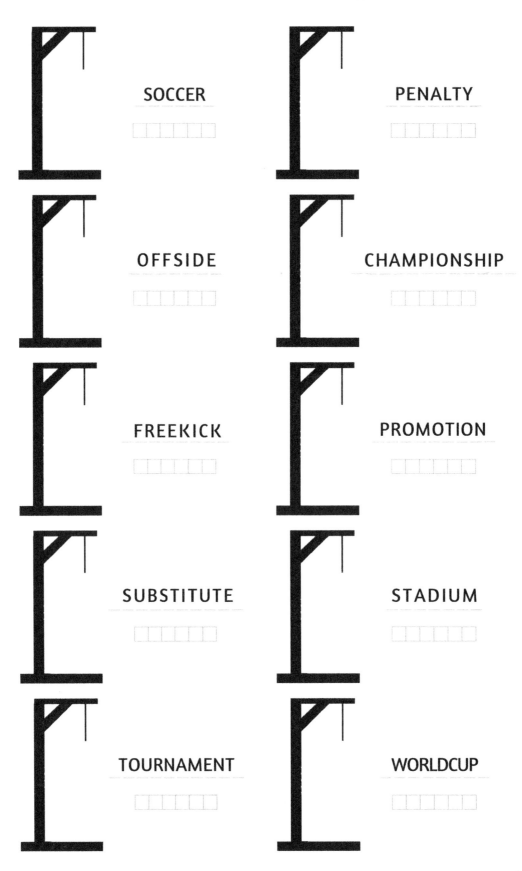

SOCCER

PENALTY

OFFSIDE

CHAMPIONSHIP

FREEKICK

PROMOTION

SUBSTITUTE

STADIUM

TOURNAMENT

WORLDCUP

Drawing Fun!

Use the gridded paper to make a copy of the Footballer

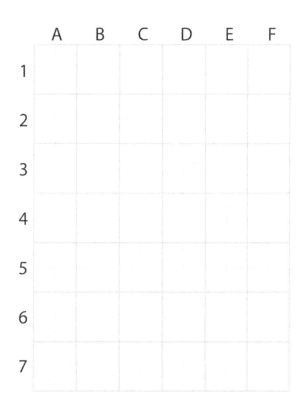

Design Football boots

Create your own design of an awesome pair of Football boots

Design Football Shirts

Design 4 different kinds of Football shirts.
Think about using different logos, colours
and styles like hoops an stripes

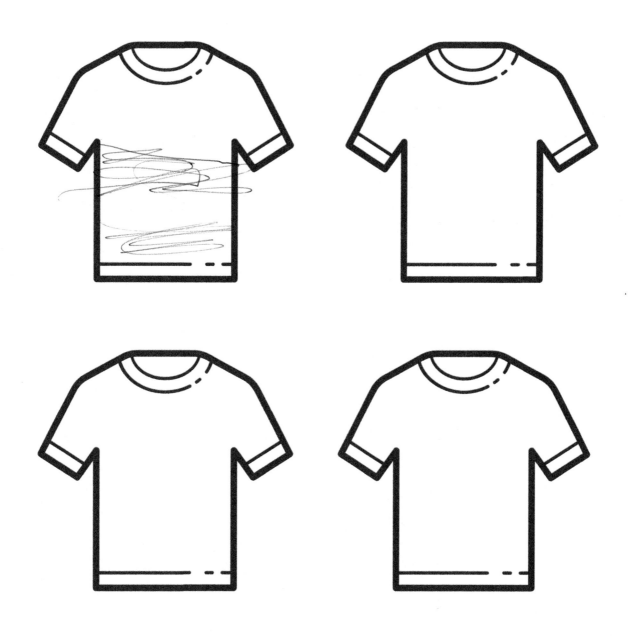

Anagrams #2

Rearrange the letters to find the names of current England players

AKHRRANYE

....

AYABOSKUK

....

CEDRICLANE

....

GAMAYHURRIER

....

ANSWERS ON PAGE 91/92

Wordsearch #3
Find these Football teams

R	N	W	V	M	F	H	Q	C	T	G	F	B	L	F	F	J	X
B	K	N	M	I	V	V	G	A	T	E	M	A	N	U	T	D	F
R	P	M	E	C	W	P	M	Q	E	I	Y	M	E	L	L	C	S
I	M	E	T	F	C	H	J	O	L	S	H	O	W	H	H	M	K
G	S	W	P	N	M	Q	D	C	D	L	W	A	C	A	M	I	N
H	S	A	Q	A	F	W	Z	X	B	B	M	S	A	M	Y	W	I
T	J	B	O	E	C	C	I	X	S	Y	O	T	S	D	N	C	L
O	J	L	E	X	O	Z	X	M	E	B	K	O	T	I	V	X	N
N	H	W	W	N	R	Z	H	U	S	G	B	N	L	N	E	I	M
C	R	H	Y	K	X	X	Q	I	V	T	D	V	E	E	W	V	Q
H	S	C	O	H	X	X	V	H	F	P	T	I	N	I	U	N	D
E	C	W	P	G	O	W	E	X	N	G	H	L	I	D	W	I	Z
L	X	I	C	R	Y	S	T	A	L	P	A	L	A	C	E	T	S
S	K	A	B	L	T	O	T	T	E	N	H	A	M	U	S	B	B
E	Z	P	B	I	C	V	K	A	R	S	E	N	A	L	T	E	X
A	Q	E	P	J	T	W	A	M	A	N	C	I	T	Y	H	J	U
X	J	L	Q	E	G	F	E	S	V	P	X	Y	W	O	A	H	U
L	I	V	E	R	P	O	O	L	Q	O	S	Z	D	B	M	J	A

MANUTD	FULHAM	ARSENAL
CHELSEA	MANCITY	BRIGHTON
WEST HAM	LIVERPOOL	TOTTENHAM
NEWCASTLE	ASTONVILLA	CRYSTALPALACE

Wordsearch #3 Solution

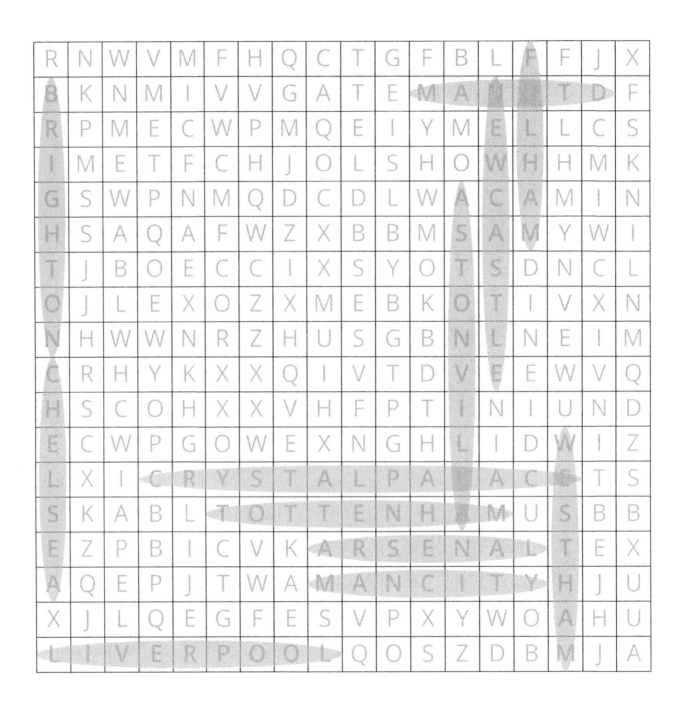

R	N	W	V	M	F	H	Q	C	T	G	F	B	L	F	F	J	X
B	K	N	M	I	V	V	G	A	T	E	M	A	I	T	D	F
R	P	M	E	C	W	P	M	Q	E	I	Y	M	E	L	L	C	S
I	M	E	T	F	C	H	J	O	L	S	H	O	W	H	H	M	K
G	S	W	P	N	M	Q	D	C	D	L	W	A	C	A	M	I	N
H	S	A	Q	A	F	W	Z	X	B	B	M	S	A	M	Y	W	I
T	J	B	O	E	C	C	I	X	S	Y	O	T	S	D	N	C	L
O	J	L	E	X	O	Z	X	M	E	B	K	O	T	I	V	X	N
N	H	W	W	N	R	Z	H	U	S	G	B	N	L	N	E	I	M
C	R	H	Y	K	X	X	Q	I	V	T	D	V	E	E	W	V	Q
H	S	C	O	H	X	X	V	H	F	P	T	I	N	I	U	N	D
E	C	W	P	G	O	W	E	X	N	G	H	L	I	D	W	I	Z
L	X	I	C	R	Y	S	T	A	L	P	A	A	C	E	T	S
S	K	A	B	L	T	O	T	T	E	N	H	M	U	S	B	B
E	Z	P	B	I	C	V	K	A	R	S	E	N	A	L	T	E	X
A	Q	E	P	J	T	W	A	M	A	N	C	I	T	Y	H	J	U
X	J	L	Q	E	G	F	E	S	V	P	X	Y	W	O	A	H	U
L	I	V	E	R	P	O	O	L	Q	O	S	Z	D	B	M	J	A

MANUTD   FULHAM   ARSENAL
CHELSEA   MANCITY   BRIGHTON
WEST HAM   LIVERPOOL   TOTTENHAM
NEWCASTLE   ASTONVILLA   CRYSTALPALACE

Did you know?

Fun Facts #1

The highest attendance for a soccer match is 199,854.

The game was the 1950 World Cup final between Brazil and Uruguay held at Maracana Stadium in Rio de Janeiro.

Who am I? #1

1. I was born on June 24, 1987, in Rosario, Argentina.
2. My debut for the senior national team was in 2005.
3. I spent over 20 years at a Catalan club before making a surprising move in 2021.
4. My nickname is "La Pulga" due to my short stature and agility.

Crossword #2

Across
1. THE COUNTRY THAT WON THE WORLD CUP IN 2014. (7 LETTERS)
5. THE PLAYER WHO HAS WON FIVE BALLON D'OR AWARDS AND IS OFTEN COMPARED TO MESSI. (7 LETTERS)
6. MAJOR INTERNATIONAL TOURNAMENT FOR EUROPEAN COUNTRIES. (5 LETTERS)
7. THE ACT OF SCORING THREE GOALS IN A SINGLE GAME. (8 LETTERS)
8. ENGLISH CLUB WHOSE NICKNAME IS "THE RED DEVILS". (9 LETTERS)
10. SOCCER'S WORLD GOVERNING BODY. (4 LETTERS)

Down
2. POPULAR SPANISH CLUB KNOWN FOR ITS RIVALRY WITH REAL MADRID. (8 LETTERS)
3. THE NUMBER OF PLAYERS IN A STANDARD SOCCER TEAM, EXCLUDING SUBSTITUTES. (5 LETTERS)
4. FAMOUS ITALIAN STADIUM LOCATED IN TURIN. (8 LETTERS)
1. THE POSITION THAT WEARS GLOVES AND CAN USE THEIR HANDS INSIDE THE BOX. (9 LETTERS)
9. THE ITEM REFEREES USE TO BOOK PLAYERS FOR SERIOUS INFRACTIONS. (9 LETTERS)
11. THE COUNTRY KNOWN AS THE "SAMBA KINGS" DUE TO THEIR FLAIR IN SOCCER. (6 LETTERS)

Crossword #2 Solution

Across
1. THE COUNTRY THAT WON THE WORLD CUP IN 2014. (7 LETTERS)
5. THE PLAYER WHO HAS WON FIVE BALLON D'OR AWARDS AND IS OFTEN COMPARED TO MESSI. (7 LETTERS)
6. MAJOR INTERNATIONAL TOURNAMENT FOR EUROPEAN COUNTRIES. (5 LETTERS)
7. THE ACT OF SCORING THREE GOALS IN A SINGLE GAME. (8 LETTERS)
8. ENGLISH CLUB WHOSE NICKNAME IS "THE RED DEVILS". (9 LETTERS)
10. SOCCER'S WORLD GOVERNING BODY. (4 LETTERS)

Down
2. POPULAR SPANISH CLUB KNOWN FOR ITS RIVALRY WITH REAL MADRID. (8 LETTERS)
3. THE NUMBER OF PLAYERS IN A STANDARD SOCCER TEAM, EXCLUDING SUBSTITUTES. (5 LETTERS)
4. FAMOUS ITALIAN STADIUM LOCATED IN TURIN. (8 LETTERS)
1. THE POSITION THAT WEARS GLOVES AND CAN USE THEIR HANDS INSIDE THE BOX. (9 LETTERS)
9. THE ITEM REFEREES USE TO BOOK PLAYERS FOR SERIOUS INFRACTIONS. (9 LETTERS)
11. THE COUNTRY KNOWN AS THE "SAMBA KINGS" DUE TO THEIR FLAIR IN SOCCER. (6 LETTERS)

Colouring Page #6

BLANK FOR COLOURING PAGE

Maze #2

Maze #2 Solution

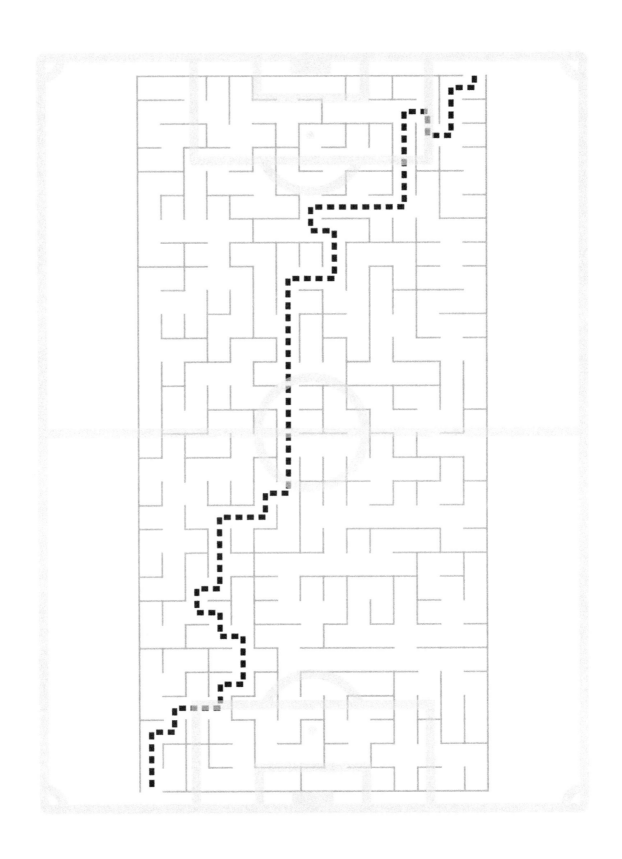

Colouring Page #7

BLANK FOR COLOURING PAGE

Match up! #1

Draw lines to match the teams to their stadiums

Chelsea   Old Trafford

Liverpool   Camp Nou

Bayern Munich   San Siro

Man United   Stamford Bridge

Barcelona   Emirates Stadium

Inter Milan   Allianz Arena

Arsenal   Anfield

Did you know?

Fun Facts #2

The longest soccer match ever lasted for 108 hours, 2 minutes, and was played to raise funds for the Tackle Africa charity.

Wordsearch #4

U	A	U	R	E	L	E	G	A	T	I	O	N	N	P
P	K	V	A	F	X	B	F	N	Y	C	L	U	B	R
G	F	P	R	O	M	O	T	I	O	N	B	M	Q	D
S	T	J	T	R	A	N	S	F	E	R	H	X	P	K
R	U	F	E	M	J	O	X	K	S	K	V	F	X	L
D	A	E	C	A	B	D	Y	W	U	X	S	N	G	K
C	O	U	N	T	E	R	J	I	P	U	M	Y	Q	I
F	O	Q	L	I	U	L	A	N	P	K	G	L	B	Z
Y	S	U	E	O	N	A	N	G	O	Y	E	U	L	Y
R	C	Y	P	N	D	L	X	B	R	Z	C	C	I	X
K	O	F	L	J	E	E	Z	A	T	L	L	I	E	I
S	C	L	E	A	R	A	N	C	E	K	F	M	D	J
J	M	E	G	S	D	G	B	K	R	U	K	J	L	X
T	Z	L	R	X	O	U	Z	K	S	H	T	G	F	N
V	H	B	L	B	G	E	O	W	N	G	O	A	L	B

Club   League   Counter
Wingback   Transfer   Own Goal
Underdog   Promotion   Formation
Clearance   Relegation   Supporters

49

Wordsearch #4 Solution

U	A	U	R	E	L	E	G	A	T	I	O	N	N	P
P	K	V	A	F	X	B	F	N	Y	C	L	U	B	R
G	F	P	R	I	M	O	T	I	O	N	B	M	Q	D
S	T	J	T	R	A	N	S	F	E	R	H	X	P	K
R	U	F	E	M	J	O	X	K	S	K	V	F	X	L
D	A	E	C	A	B	D	Y	W	U	X	S	N	G	K
C	O	U	N	T	E	R	J	I	P	U	M	Y	Q	I
F	O	Q	L	I	U	L	A	N	P	K	G	L	B	Z
Y	S	U	E	O	N	A	N	G	O	Y	E	U	L	Y
R	C	Y	P	N	D	L	X	B	R	Z	C	C	I	X
K	O	F	L	J	E	E	Z	A	T	L	L	I	E	I
S	C	L	E	A	R	A	N	C	E	K	F	M	D	J
J	M	E	G	S	D	G	B	K	R	U	K	J	L	X
T	Z	L	R	X	O	U	Z	K	S	H	T	G	F	N
V	H	B	L	B	G	E	O	W	N	G	O	A	L	B

Club   League   Counter
Wingback   Transfer   Own Goal
Underdog   Promotion   Formation
Clearance   Relegation   Supporters

Matchday Maths #1

 = 3

 = 6

 = 9

 + = 9

 X = 54

 / = 3

$$3\overline{)9}^{\,3}$$

Draw their Shirt

Draw and Colour the 4 shirts in the style of the names underneath them

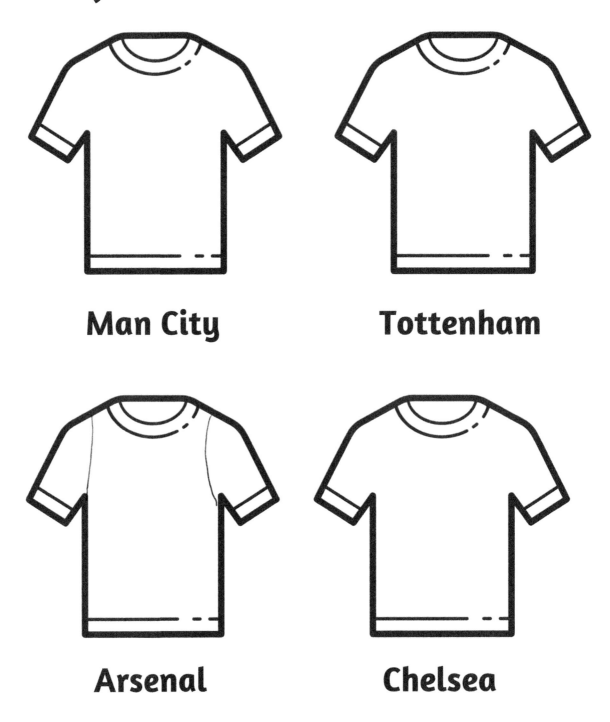

Man City

Tottenham

Arsenal

Chelsea

Crossword #3

Across
1. CLUB THAT PLAYS AT SELHURST PARK (6 LETTERS)
5. EGYPTIAN FORWARD WHO HAS DAZZLED FOR LIVERPOOL. (5 LETTERS)
6. TRADITIONAL COLOR OF THE TOFFEES, EVERTON'S HOME KIT. (4 LETTERS)
9. CLUB NICKNAMED THE "RED DEVILS". (6 LETTERS)
10. CLUB KNOWN FOR ITS ANTHEM "YOU'LL NEVER WALK ALONE". (8 LETTERS)
12. TEAM THAT PLAYS AT ST. JAMES' PARK. (9 LETTERS)

Down
2. STADIUM THAT'S HOME TO WEST HAM UNITED. (6 LETTERS)
3. 2004-2005 PREMIER LEAGUE WINNERS UNDER MOURINHO. (7 LETTERS)
4. SEAGULLS IS THE NICKNAME FOR THIS PREMIER LEAGUE CLUB. (8 LETTERS)
7. THE ANIMAL THAT REPRESENTS THE PREMIER LEAGUE TROPHY. (4 LETTERS)
8. NORTH LONDON CLUB RIVALING ARSENAL. (9 LETTERS)
11. 2015-2016 SURPRISE PREMIER LEAGUE WINNERS. (9 LETTERS)

Crossword #3

Across
1. CLUB THAT PLAYS AT SELHURST PARK (6 LETTERS)
5. EGYPTIAN FORWARD WHO HAS DAZZLED FOR LIVERPOOL. (5 LETTERS)
6. TRADITIONAL COLOR OF THE TOFFEES, EVERTON'S HOME KIT. (4 LETTERS)
9. CLUB NICKNAMED THE "RED DEVILS". (6 LETTERS)
10. CLUB KNOWN FOR ITS ANTHEM "YOU'LL NEVER WALK ALONE". (8 LETTERS)
12. TEAM THAT PLAYS AT ST. JAMES' PARK. (9 LETTERS)

Down
2. STADIUM THAT'S HOME TO WEST HAM UNITED. (6 LETTERS)
3. 2004-2005 PREMIER LEAGUE WINNERS UNDER MOURINHO. (7 LETTERS)
4. SEAGULLS IS THE NICKNAME FOR THIS PREMIER LEAGUE CLUB. (8 LETTERS)
7. THE ANIMAL THAT REPRESENTS THE PREMIER LEAGUE TROPHY. (4 LETTERS)
8. NORTH LONDON CLUB RIVALING ARSENAL. (9 LETTERS)
11. 2015-2016 SURPRISE PREMIER LEAGUE WINNERS. (9 LETTERS)

Match up! #2

Draw lines to match the Stadiums to their Countries

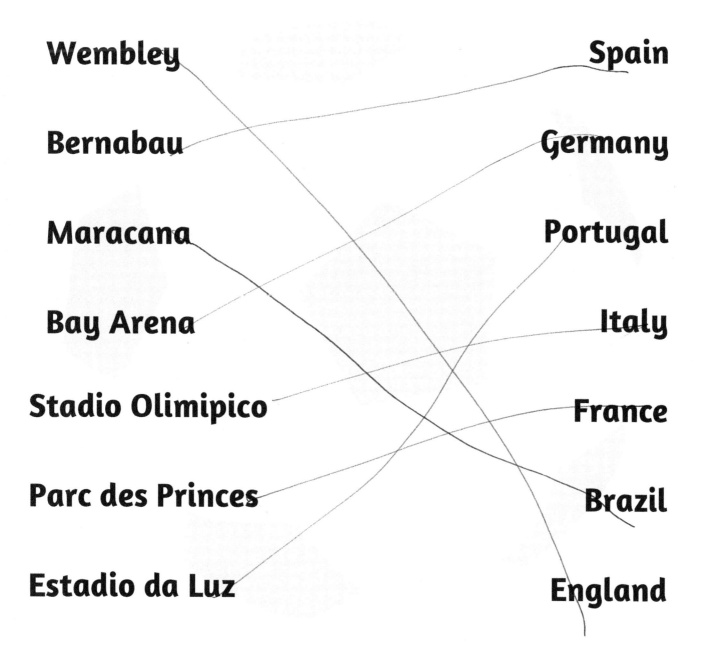

Wembley   Spain

Bernabau   Germany

Maracana   Portugal

Bay Arena   Italy

Stadio Olimipico   France

Parc des Princes   Brazil

Estadio da Luz   England

Create a formation
Use your imagination to create your own football formation. How many defenders, midfielders and strikers does it have? What is it called?

Formation name: 5-1-4

11
Eusébio

10
Cantona

18
Van Basten

9
Pelé

7
Zidane

3
Roberto
Carlos

21
Koeman

4
Blanc

8
5
Cannavaro

66
Alexander-
Arnold

Yashin

Matchday Maths #2

 = 2

 = 4

 = 5

 X = 8

 X = 20

 + = 7

ANSWERS ON PAGE 91/92

Did you know?

Fun Facts #3

The only World Cup tournaments where no player received a red card were in 1970 in Mexico and 1950 in Brazil.

Match up! #3

Draw lines to match the Players to their Nations

Jude Bellingham   Argentina

Lionel Messi   Egypt

Christiano Ronaldo   Brazil

Neymar Jr.   England

Kylian Mbappe   Portugal

Mohamed Salah   France

Who am I? #2

1. I was born on October 28, 1974, in Santiago, Chile.
2. I've managed teams in Argentina, Mexico, Spain, and England.
3. My intense style of pressing and attacking football has earned me praise and success.
4. As of my last known appointment in 2021, I manage a Premier League club known for its sky blue jerseys.

ANSWERS ON PAGE 91/92

Colouring Page #8

BLANK FOR COLOURING PAGE

Name the Club #1

1. I was founded in 1897.
2. My nickname is 'La Vecchia Signora' which means Old Lady.
3. We play at the Allianz Stadium.
4. We have won the Champions League trophy many times and have had players like Christiano Ronaldo play for us.

Bayern/
Juventus

Did you know?

Fun Facts #4

The world's oldest football club is Sheffield FC from England, founded in 1857.

Matchday Maths #3

 = 3

 = 10

 = 5

 X = 36

 / = $5\overline{)10}^{\,2}$

 + = 8

$18\overline{)64}$

Anagrams #3

Rearrange the letters to find the names of these International players

ELISIONELMS (ARGENTINA)

Lionel Messi
....

AMBYKIPPLANE (FRANCE)

Kylian Mbappé
....

RONICASHIRL (BRAZIL)

....

HUMSMARTELLO (GERMANY)

....

Draw a stadium

Use the space below to draw and colour your own football stadium

BLANK FOR COLOURING PAGE

Wordsearch #5

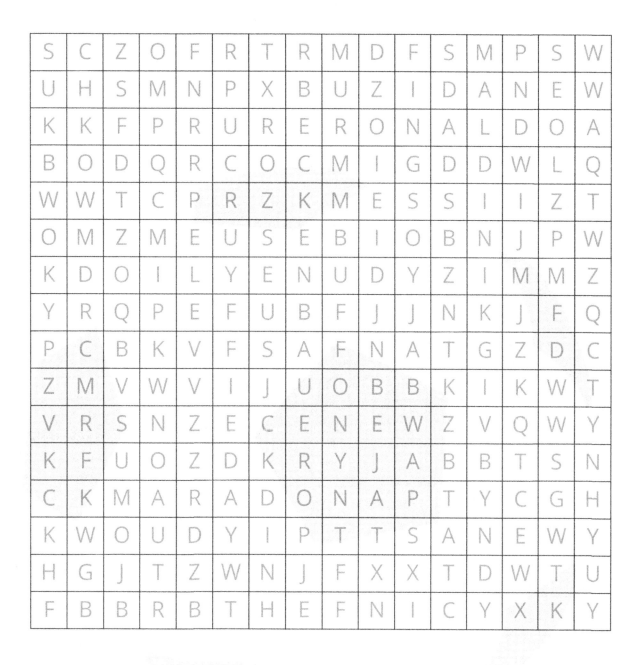

S	C	Z	O	F	R	T	R	M	D	F	S	M	P	S	W
U	H	S	M	N	P	X	B	U	Z	I	D	A	N	E	W
K	K	F	P	R	U	R	E	R	O	N	A	L	D	O	A
B	O	D	Q	R	C	O	C	M	I	G	D	D	W	L	Q
W	W	T	C	P	R	Z	K	M	E	S	S	I	I	Z	T
O	M	Z	M	E	U	S	E	B	I	O	B	N	J	P	W
K	D	O	I	L	Y	E	N	U	D	Y	Z	I	M	M	Z
Y	R	Q	P	E	F	U	B	F	J	J	N	K	J	F	Q
P	C	B	K	V	F	S	A	F	N	A	T	G	Z	D	C
Z	M	V	W	V	I	J	U	O	B	B	K	I	K	W	T
V	R	S	N	Z	E	C	E	N	E	W	Z	V	Q	W	Y
K	F	U	O	Z	D	K	R	Y	J	A	B	B	T	S	N
C	K	M	A	R	A	D	O	N	A	P	T	Y	C	G	H
K	W	O	U	D	Y	I	P	T	T	S	A	N	E	W	Y
H	G	J	T	Z	W	N	J	F	X	X	T	D	W	T	U
F	B	B	R	B	T	H	E	F	N	I	C	Y	X	K	Y

Pele   Messi   Cruyff
Zidane   Buffon   Ronaldo
Maldini   Eusebio   Maradona
Beckenbauer

Wordsearch #5 Solution

S	C	Z	O	F	R	T	R	M	D	F	S	M	P	S	W
U	H	S	M	N	P	X	B	U	Z	I	D	A	N	E	W
K	K	F	P	R	U	R	E	R	O	N	A	L	D	O	A
B	O	D	Q	R	C	O	C	M	I	G	D	D	W	L	Q
W	W	T	C	P	R	Z	K	M	E	S	S	I	I	Z	T
O	M	Z	M	S	S	B	A	I	O	B	N	J	P	W
K	D	O	I	L	Y	E	N	U	D	Y	Z	I	M	M	Z
Y	R	Q	P	E	F	U	B	F	J	J	N	K	J	F	Q
P	C	B	K	V	F	S	A	F	N	A	T	G	Z	D	C
Z	M	V	W	V	I	J	U	O	B	B	K	I	K	W	T
V	R	S	N	Z	E	C	E	N	E	W	Z	V	Q	W	Y
K	F	U	O	Z	D	K	R	Y	J	A	B	B	T	S	N
C	K	M	A	R	A	D	O	N	A	P	T	Y	C	G	H
K	W	O	U	D	Y	I	P	T	T	S	A	N	E	W	Y
H	G	J	T	Z	W	N	J	F	X	X	T	D	W	T	U
F	B	B	R	B	T	H	E	F	N	I	C	Y	X	K	Y

Pele
Zidane
Maldini
Beckenbauer

Messi
Buffon
Eusebio

Cruyff
Ronaldo
Maradona

Colouring Page #9

BLANK FOR COLOURING PAGE

Anagrams #4

Rearrange the letters to find the names of these famous players

LEEP (BRAZIL)

...... *Pele* ....

BOEIUSE (PORTUGAL)

...... *Eusebio* ....

DURLEGMERL (GERMANY)

...... *Gerd Müller* ....

ABBRBLOCHTONY (ENGLAND)

...... *Bobby charlton* ....

NAME YOUR FAVOURITE STADIUM

....

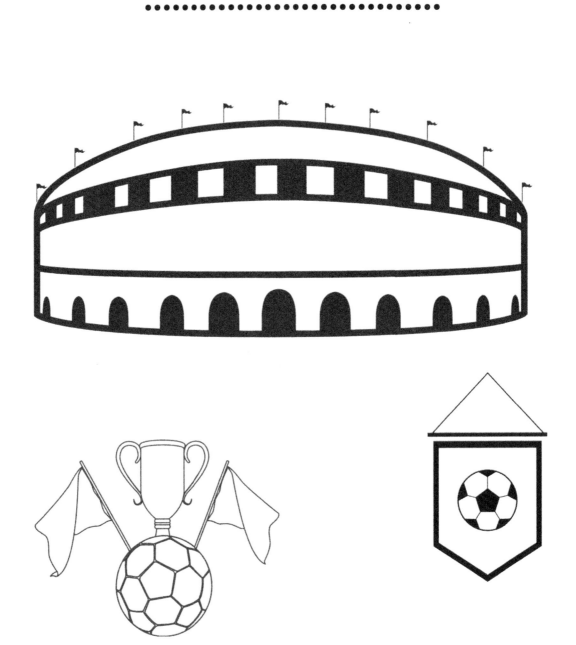

NAME A MATCH
YOU WANT TO SEE

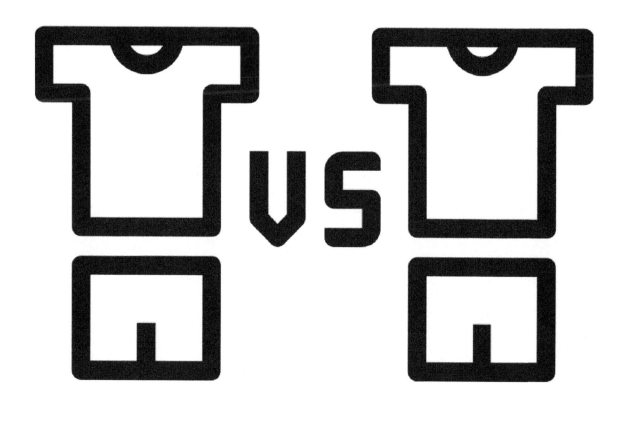

··   ··

NOW COLOUR THE STRIPS TO MATCH THE
TEAMS COLOURS

BLANK FOR COLOURING PAGE

FIND THE BOOTS

NAME A FAMOUS COACH

....

COLOUR YOUR KIT

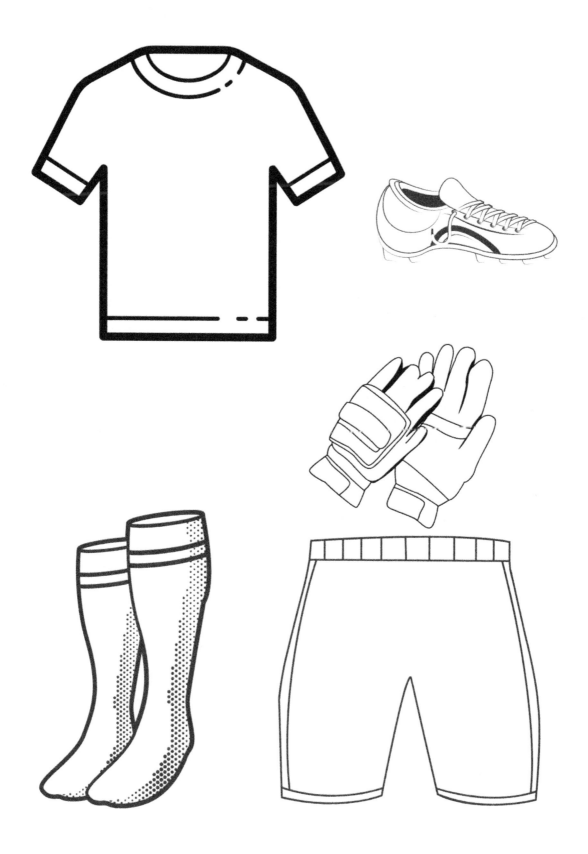

BLANK FOR COLOURING PAGE

Personalise your shirt

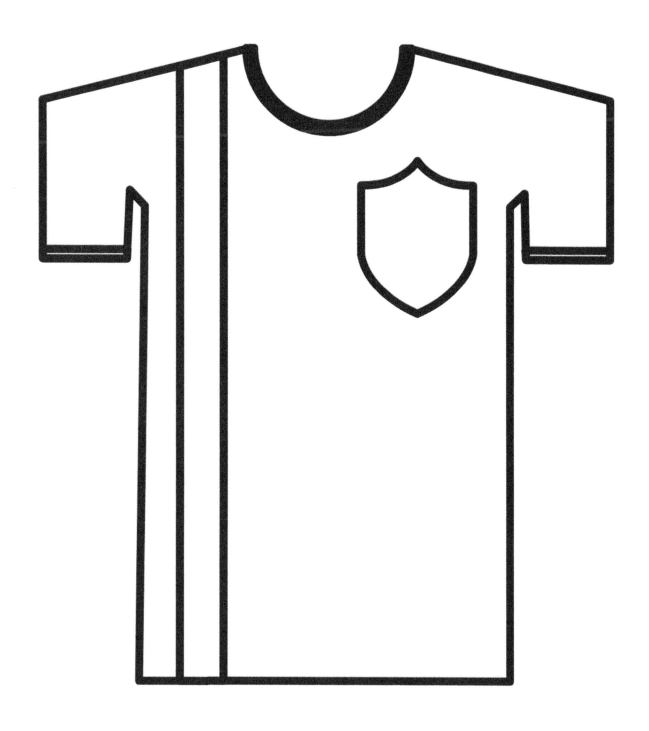

BLANK FOR COLOURING PAGE

MATCHDAY!! - A free football game

This is a simple and fun Football game that you can play on your own or with your friends or family.

It uses a single six sided dice that you can find in board games or hobby shops.

HOW TO PLAY

Write down the names of the 2 teams to play in the game.

Each half of the game has 20 main dice rolls on this table.

Matchday - The game

MAIN TABLE

1 TACKLE

2 CORNER

3 PASS

4 TACKLE

5 SHOOT

6 PASS

A team keeps possession with a pass or corner result and loses possession with a tackle result. If a shot result comes up then roll on the shot table.

SHOT TABLE

1 MISS

2 MISS

3 FOUL

4 GOAL

5 MISS

6 GOAL

Matchday - the game

The game goes back to the main table with the other team in possession if the result is a miss or a goal.

If the result is a foul then roll on the foul table and the set piece table to determine the outcome of the Free kick / Penalty.

FOUL TABLE	SET PIECE TABLE
1 FREE KICK	1 GOAL
2 FREE KICK	2 GOAL
3 FREE KICK	3 GOAL
4 FREE KICK	4 MISS
5 PENALTY	5 MISS
6 PENALTY	6 MISS

The game then returns to the main table once again. Each half lasts 20 rolls on the main table (the highlights) and then game is over.

Matchday - the game

GAMEPLAY EXAMPLE

In my fictional league, Hull United take on the Manchester Rebels. Hull will start with the ball.

ROLL 1 - TACKLE Possession goes to the Rebels
ROLL 2 - PASS Rebels keep the ball
ROLL 3 - SHOOT. Roll on the shot table, a 4, GOAL!!! Its 1-0 to the Rebels. Back to Hulls ball.

ROLL 4 - CORNER. Hull applying pressure
ROLL 5 - SHOT. Roll on the shot table, a 3, FOUL. Roll on the foul table, a 4, FREE KICK. Hull have a chance here. Roll on the set piece table, a 5, MISS!! Just wide. Now back to the main table for ROLL 6 with the Rebels.

And so on....

Play your own league

Teams

1 Hartle port V

2 Hartle port (

3 Bromley

4 Maidstone V

5 Port salle

6 Vale Pool

2

1. Manchester United
2. Man City   Chelsea
3. Arsenal
4. Liverpool
5. Aston Villa
6. Ipswich

Enter the names of six teams to play in your league in the table above.

Now enter the team names next to each number in the fixture lists on the next few pages. These will become the fixtures for your very own league.

What is your league called?

National EL5   NEL5

NEL CHAMPIO

English Premier League

SPL
Cinch
Scottish
Prem

87

Matchday - fixtures

Round 1

1	2	3	U	6		5	2	-
2	2 1		U	5	5	4		-
3	2 2		U	4	3		3	-

Round 2

6	4	1	U	4	1	2	-
5	2	3	U	3	0	2	-
1	5	4	U	2	2 1		-

Round 3

2	4 4	U	6	1 3	-
3	0	U	1	3	-
4	1	U	5	2	-

Round 4

6	0	U	5	5	-
1	5	U	4	1	-
2	3	U	3	2	-

3

1 Portsalle 9 pts GD 7
2 vallepool md 4 pts 0
3 Maidston U 4 pts -1
4
5
6

2

1 Portsalle 9 pts GD 7
2 Maidstone U 4 pts 0
3 vallepool 4 pts -1
4
5
6

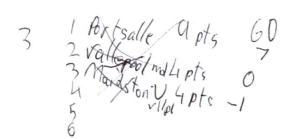

Matchday - fixtures

Round 5

3 *2* v 6 *3* -
4 *2* v 2 *1* -
5 *5* v 1 *2* -

Round 6

6 *1* v 3 *2* -
2 *2* v 4 *2* -
1 *8* v 5 *3* -

Round 7

5 *4* v 6 *5* -
4 *0* v 1 *1* -
3 *2* v 2 *3* -

Round 8

6 *3* v 2 *4* -
1 *1* v 3 *0* -
5 *2* v 4 *1* -

Matchday - fixtures

Round 9

4	4	U	6	4	-
3	4	U	5	4	-
2	4	U	1	4	-

Round 10

6	3	U	1	1	-
5	4	U	2	1	-
4	1	U	3	2	-

Play each game using the rules provided and record the scores. Give 3 points for a win and 1 for a draw. Once completed, fill out the league table below to determine the winner.

	TEAM	P	W	D	L	GF	GA	GD	PTS
1	~~Vattepool~~ Portsalle	10	7	1	2	36	23	13	22
2	Hartlepol United	10	6	1	3	32	23	9	19
3	~~Vattepool~~ Hartlepool City	10	4	2	4	25	27	-2	14
4	Vallepool	10	4	2	4	26	30	-4	14
5	Maidstone United	10	2	3	5	16	22	-6	9
6	Bromley	10	2	1	7	16	25	-9	7

Promoted -1
To NLeague-2
Play-offs
3

Relegated to NL5 6
Mdstn

GF GA GD
HC 25 27 -2
VP 26 30 -4

MaidstnV 2win 9 Val 8win 22 Portsl 4win 14

HrlplV 4win 9 HartlepoolC 4win 14 Brom 2win 7

90

Answers

Anagrams #1

LIVERPOOL, LUTON TOWN, BOURNEMOUTH, TOTTENHAM

Anagrams #2

Harry Kane, Bukayo Saka, Declan Rice, Harry Maguire

Who am I? #1

Lionel Messi

Match up #1

Chelsea = Stamford Bridge, Liverpool = Anfield, Bayern Munich = Allianz Arena, Man United = Old Trafford, Barcelona = Camp Nou, Inter Milan = San Siro, Arsenal = Emirates Stadium

Matchday maths #1

9, 54, 3

Match up #2

Wemley = England, Bernabau = Spain, Maracana = Brazil, Bay Arena = Germany, Stadio Olimpico = Italy, Parc des Princes = France, Estadio da Luz = Portugal

Matchday maths #2

8,20, 7

Answers

Match up #3

Jude Bellingham = England, Lionel Messi = Argentina, Christiano Ronaldo = Portugal, Neymar Jr. = Brazil, Kylian Mbappe = France, Mohamed Salah = Egypt

Who am I? #2

Pep Guardiola

Name the Club #1

Juventus

Matchday maths #3

30, 2, 8

Anagrams #3

Lionel Messi, Kylian Mbappe, Richarlison, Thomas Muller

Anagrams #4

Pele, Eusebio, Gerd Muller, Bobby Charlton

Printed in Great Britain
by Amazon

36440992R00053